Patagonia
WILD LAND AT THE END OF THE EARTH

TIM HAUF

Text by Conger Beasley Jr.
Foreword by Gregory Crouch

Patagonia: Wild Land at the End of the Earth
Photography by Tim Hauf
Text by Conger Beasley Jr.
Edited by Cheryl Carnahan
Book design by Gretchen Scoble Design

Copyright © 2004 by Tim Hauf Photography. All rights reserved. No part of this publication may be reproduced, stored in a retrieval system, or transmitted, in any form or by any means, electronic, mechanical, recorded, photocopied, graphic, or otherwise, without the prior written permission of Tim Hauf Photography. Published by Tim Hauf Photography, P.O. Box 1241, Kingston, WA 98346.

Visit my web site at **www.timhaufphotography.com** or email me at **timhauf@hotmail.com** for information on ordering additional copies, or for information on photo usage rights or for photo enlargements.

Library of Congress Catalog Number: 2003098724

ISBN: 0-9720743-3-3

First Printing June 2004
Printed and bound in Korea

Patagonia has not been widely photographed. I had no mental image of it,

only the fanciful blur of legend, the giants on the shore, the ostrich on the plain,

and a sense of displaced people, like my own ancestors who had fled from Europe.

When I tried to call up an image of Patagonia, nothing came and I was as helpless

as if I had tried to describe the landscape of a distant planet or paint the smell of an onion.

The unknown landscape is justification enough for going to it.

BRUCE CHATWIN & PAUL THEROUX
Patagonia Revisited (1986)

ng light, Lago Pehoe with Paine Grande and Cuernos del Paine in background.

Table of Contents

Foreword
by Gregory Crouch

9

INTRODUCTION
Land's End

11

CHAPTER 1
Distant Horizons

15

CHAPTER 2
Torres del Paine National Park

29

CHAPTER 3
Los Glaciares National Park

109

CHAPTER 4
Tierra del Fuego

143

GLOSSARY 167

BIBLIOGRAPHY 168

Cuernos del Paine and Towers of the Frenchman.

Foreword

By Gregory Crouch

EXPLORERS, ADVENTURERS, FORTUNE SEEKERS, SETTLERS, OUTLAWS, AND OUTCASTS HAVE BEEN captivated by the otherworldly landscapes of Patagonia ever since Magellan first cast anchor into the waters of Bahiá San Julian in 1520. Patagonia is a land of strange magic and power, a region of wind-wracked steppes, wild rivers and forests, enormous glaciers, incomparable mountains, and keen, algid air. Shared by Argentina and Chile at the extreme southern end of the American continents, Patagonia stands squarely athwart what sailors refer to as the "roaring forties" and "furious fifties"–that region of the Southern Hemisphere known for ferocious winds and storms.

For most of the past dozen years, I have been a human comet in long orbits around the great peaks of Patagonia. I have climbed many mountains in Patagonia and failed on many others. Seven times I've made the pilgrimage, and I will go back, for the times I spend in those mountains are the most charged moments of my life. The Patagonian Andes have taught me most of what I know about terror and joy, friendship, mirth and gravity, courage and cowardice and when to take a risk, success and failure, persistence, patience, endurance, and opportunity. To them I owe my most extreme visions of beauty and most of what I know about myself. Whenever I pull Patagonia into my mind, which I do many times a day, I see a vision of the great peaks as they soar up into a sky full of angry clouds. I hear the terrible wind. And I feel fear.

The Patagonian gauntlet of hardship cannot be evaded. It is a brutal, unforgiving place, trapped between angry torrents of sea and sky. The region's history is a litany of suffering, but now, more than ever, mankind needs such savage, unfettered landscapes to hold our dreams.

GREGORY CROUCH, author of *Enduring Patagonia,* is Field Director of Conservacion Patagonicas (formerly The Patagonia Land Trust), a nonprofit foundation dedicated to preserving the wild natural beauty and unique biodiversity of Patagonia.

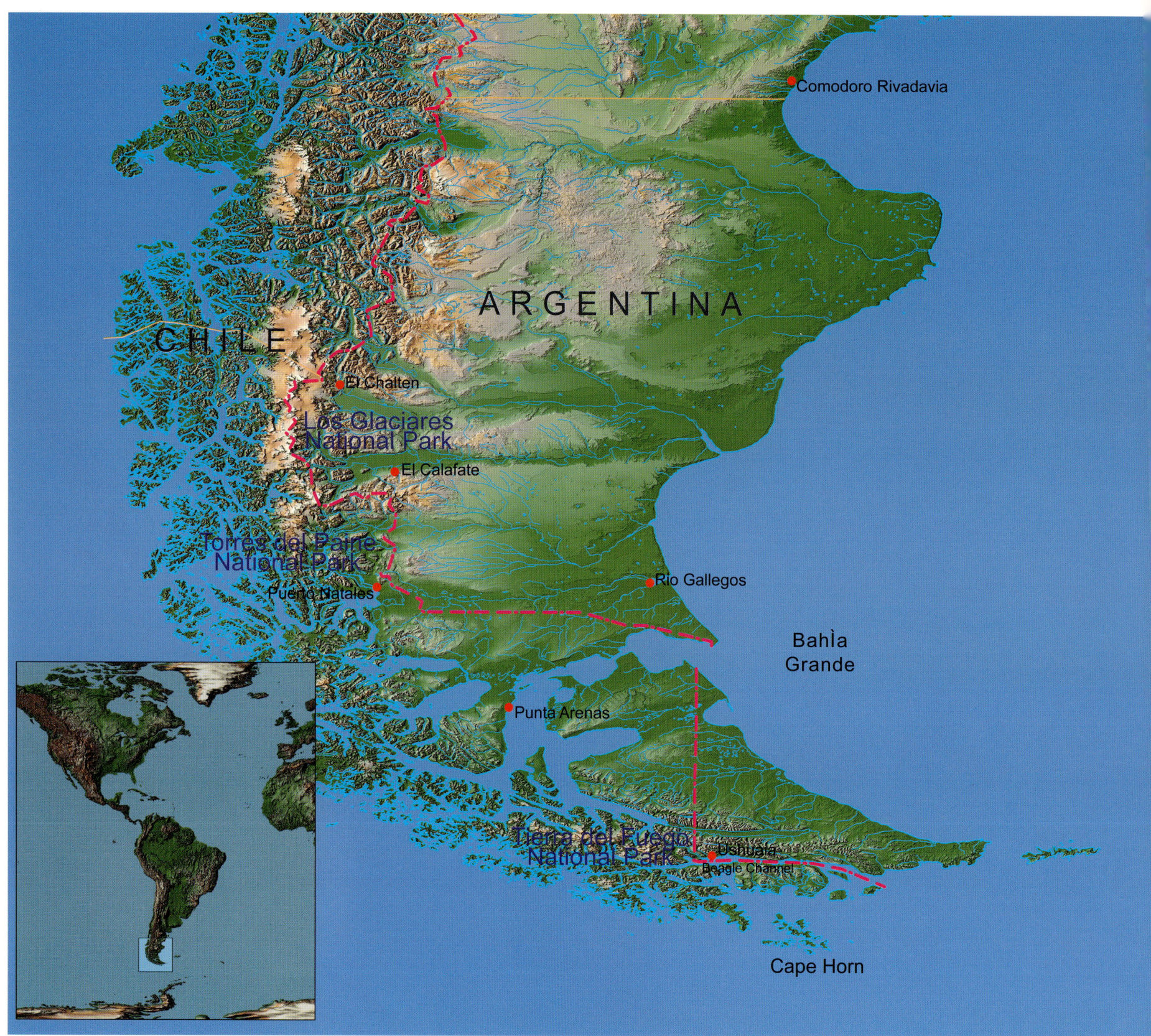

INTRODUCTION

Land's End

From Magellan's ship as it made landfall at San Julian in March 1520 on the southeast shore of what today is known as Argentina, the crew of tough, hard-bitten Spanish sailors saw what appeared to be a human monster with gigantic feet dancing naked on the sand. The monster leaped and howled and threw sticks in the air. As the white men approached, he jabbed a finger at the sky, as if to indicate that these strange, bearded creatures had somehow descended from the heavens.

The giant was a Tehuelche Indian, whom nineteenth-century Argentine explorer Ramon Lista would later single out for their extraordinary size and prowess. "Their stature is unrivalled," he wrote in 1894, "and when one cuts through past exaggerations, one can confirm that the Tehuelche is the tallest man in the world." Their height may have been accentuated by the fur robes they wore, complete with a pointed hood that added inches to their stature. Antonio Pigafetta, Magellan's chronicler on his historic 'round-the-world voyage, claims these "giants" ran faster than horses, ate raw flesh, lived in tents, and wandered around the countryside like gypsies. The story goes that when Magellan himself first espied the dancing figure he said, "Ha! Patagon!" which meant "Big Foot," because of the size of his foot. *Pata* means a foot in Spanish; *gonia* means a roaring or gnashing of the teeth in Greek. Since Pigafetta describes the Tehuelche roaring like a bull over the steady rush of the wind, that may be why Magellan added the suffix.

But the term might also have a literary antecedent. Seven years before Magellan set out with his tiny fleet of five boats from the Spanish port of San Lucar on September 20, 1519, a romance of chivalry entitled *Primaleon of Greece* was published in Europe. The book traces the adventures of a bold knight named Primaleon, who sails to a remote island and meets a primitive people who wear animal skins and eat raw flesh. In the interior lives a monster called the Grand Patagon, with the head of a dog and the feet of a stag and a lusty appetite for women. The chief of the islanders persuades Primaleon to rid them of this nuisance. He rides out, wounds the Patagon with a single sword thrust, and binds him up with leather straps.

Primaleon decides to ship the creature back home to Polonia to add to his collection of curiosities. The queen is repulsed by the sight of the creature, but her daughter, Princess Zephira, soothes him by singing to him and teaching him her language, whereupon Patagon—disgusting, dirty, and disheveled—follows her about like a faithful dog.

Possibly inspired by this fanciful plotline, Magellan, while overwintering at San Julian, apprehended two Tehuelchan giants for his monarch, Spanish King Charles V, and his Queen Empress. The giants howled in protest at the prospect of being abducted from their native land; one eventually escaped, but Magellan managed to get the other onboard and baptize him with the name Paul. Paul died of scurvy in the Pacific, and his body was fed to the sharks. Magellan also died in the Pacific, pierced to the quick by a Filipino spear. Almost ninety years

later, in 1611, William Shakespeare's play *The Tempest* premiered in London featuring a Tehuelche-like character named Caliban, half-human, half-beast, who mouths bitter curses against the white race. Biographers know Shakespeare had read Pigafetta's account of Magellan's voyage and in all likelihood *Primaleon of Greece*. Writer Bruce Chatwin sums it up best: "I think we have a situation in which a bad novel inspired a great explorer to do something shoddy, which, in turn, inspired the greatest playwright to one of his greatest creations."

Paine Grande and Cuernos del Paine across Lago Pehoe.

CHAPTER 1

Distant Horizons

Punta Arenas (Sandy Point), a Chilean port town with a population of 100,000 located on the Magellan Straits at the tip of South America, offers a convenient entryway into the vast, imposing, "down-under" region known as Patagonia. Once a thriving entrepôt, home to early wool, cattle, lumber, and shipping magnates, Punta Arenas was originally established in 1848 as a penal colony.

The town boomed during the nineteenth century; entrepreneurs built impressive homes and mansions that today have been converted into banks and museums. In the chilly air of a cloudy spring day in early December when photographer Tim Hauf and I arrived, the city exuded the nostalgic ambiance of a more vigorous era when the streets bustled with fortune seekers and the wharves were packed with ships from all over the world.

The completion of the Panama Canal in 1914 put the quietus on the town's economic ambitions. Ships no longer had to brave the the perilous trip around Cape Horn or through one of the storm-tossed straits linking the Atlantic and Pacific Oceans to reach important markets in Europe or North America. Today, with its duty-free zone and oil revenues, Punta Arenas is enjoying a modest resurgence.

The real Patagonia begins a few miles outside the city limits with the revelation of a wide, windswept region—part tundra, part shortgrass prairie—that carries the eye with astounding ease to distant horizons, both watery and terrestrial. The penguin sanctuaries of Isla Magdalena and Seno Otway offer an opportunity to observe this remarkable creature at close range. The Magellanic penguin *(Spheniscus magellanicus),* which Antonio Pigafetta referred to as "a kind of strange goose," is one of three flightless Patagonia birds, along with the lesser rhea *(Pterocnemia pennata)* (a type of ostrich) and the flightless steamer duck *(Tachyeres pteneres)*. The penguins, with their finlike, attenuated wings and black-and-white stripes beribboning their compact, tubular bodies, come ashore in September (the beginning of spring in these southerly latitudes). Tottery, comical creatures with a quaint upright posture, they look like party revelers in white tie and tails trying not to act drunk.

These particular penguins, one of 18 known species, are also called jackass penguins for their loud, braying calls. The males arrive at the breeding ground in September to reoccupy the same nests they inhabited the year before. Females lay two eggs in October. After about 40 days of incubation, the first "pigeons" with grayish feathers are born in November. Parents now must redouble their vigilance against predators—skunks, foxes, armadillos. A single pigeon usually survives to maturity; by the following March it is strong enough to leave the breeding ground and head out to sea for the next six months. While at sea, its natural predators include orcas, seals, and giant petrels.

< Punta Arenas.

Later that first morning I spotted my first Andean condor *(Vultur gryphus),* the second-largest bird in the world after the albatross. I saw three or four sailing over a field, huge black-and-white creatures with a sweeping wingspan and a distinctive white collar and white splash across the upper wings. Once airborne in this wind-scoured world, they rarely need to flap their wings to stay aloft.

We had lunch in Puerto Natales, a pleasant town located on the eastern edge of Last Hope Sound, a glacier-fed, turquoise-colored channel that snakes west through a maze of dark green islands to the Pacific Ocean. Gloomy gray mountains flank the sound to the west; to the east, a vast steppe (flatland) unrolls to the horizon in wide, treeless swells.

At the end of that first afternoon, as the bus approached Lago Sarmiento and the entrance to Torres del Paine National Park, the wind ripped and howled—a solid, stunning force, stiff as a starched canvas. Just outside the park we passed a small herd of guanacos *(Lama guanicoe).* Guanacos usually live between 15 and 17 years. They are related to their South American cousins—the alpaca, vicuna, and llama—though they thrive at a much lower altitude. Mating couples produce one offspring a year; gestation lasts eleven months. The animals roam about the country on padded hooves, which insulate their weight and result in less wear and tear on the fragile Patagonian grasslands.

We also see lesser rheas which roam the dry steppes of eastern Patagonia. They are similar to, but smaller than, the African ostrich, *(Struthio camelus)* to which they are distantly related. Adult rheas stand four to five feet tall. The male incubates the eggs and takes care of the chicks while the female wanders off to mate with another male to ensure that the gene pool is thoroughly mixed and disseminated.

By the end of that first day it was apparent that a totally different order of critters was to be found in these austral lands, especially in the way in which the animals came to be. Millions of years ago, Africa, India, Australia, Antarctica, and South America were all part of one continent, known as Gondwana, located in the region of the South Pole. Today, they share many similar species.

Boat harbor, Puerto Natales.

< *left:* Chilco *(Fuschia magellanica); center:* Magellanic penguin; *right:* Andean condor.

DISTANT HORIZONS 17

The most difficult and dangerous feature of navigation in the straits is the encountering of sudden and violent squalls, which strike the vessel without the least warning, and are frequently enough to wreck her in a few minutes, even in the hands of the most experienced seamen.

BENJAMIN FRANKLIN BOURNE
The Captive in Patagonia: Life Among the Giants (1853)

< Isla Magdalena Natural Monument.

Magellanic penguin.

I have already observed this state of weakness,
almost lethargy, on many previous occasions:
one becomes indifferent, insensitive, to everything:
one marches unconsciously, one neither questions
nor wonders about anything; it is as if all possibility
of thought was suspended. It is a state of insensitivity
so great that one temporarily even loses the sense of time
and space. Some may think I exaggerate,
but anyone who has journeyed in this solitude,
anyone who had ridden hour after hour under the
scorching Patagonian summer sun,
anyone who has seen time and again
the same landscape, always majestic,
but always desolate and monotonous,
will understand my observation.

RAMON LISTA
A Journey to the Southern Andes (1893)

Magellanic penguin colony, Isla Magdalena Natural Monument.

Magellanic penguin colony, Isla Magdalena Natural Monument.

Magellanic penguins in burrow, Isla Magdalena Natural Monument.

*Patagonia . . .
is the wind-blown tip
of the continent below
latitude 42 degrees,
and is split between
Chile and Argentina.
The Chilean coasts
are choked with rain forest,
but east of the Andes
there are deserts of grey-green
thornscrub and grassy pampas
that remind one
of Nevada or Wyoming.
After 1900, Patagonia actually
became an extension of the
rough-riding West:
Butch Cassidy and the Sundance Kid
came down and robbed the
Bank of Tarapaca and London
in Rio Gallegos in 1905.*

BRUCE CHATWIN
Anatomy of Restlessness (1996)

Wildflowers and horses, near Puerto Natales.

Serrano Glacier, Bernardo O'Higgins National Park.

*When alone in the calmness and warmth of my home,
I let my spirit wander astray among the memory of so many images
and adventures, the peaks of Patagonia appear before me so unreal, so fabulously shaped,
that I believe that these images have come out of some mad dream.*

LIONNEL TERRAY
member of first party to scale Mount Fitzroy, February 2, 1952

Cabanas del Paine, guest quarters just outside Torres del Paine National Park.

DISTANT HORIZONS 27

CHAPTER 2

Torres del Paine National Park

THE PAINES ARE RELATIVELY NEW MOUNTAINS COMPARED WITH THE ANDES, WHICH DATE BACK 65 TO 70 MILLION YEARS. Formation of the Andes began when the oceanic Nazca Plate crunched under the continental South American Plate, triggering a series of catastrophic eruptions that smothered the region in heaps of volcanic ash. This activity continued until approximately 2 million years ago when the Andes reached their present-day elevation. Since then ice has been the most powerful shaping force; at one point the entire cordillera and a considerable portion of the Patagonian lowlands were immured under an ice sheet many hundreds of meters deep. (Paine—"pale blue" in the Tehuelche Indian language—probably refers to the color of the nearby glacial lakes.)

The Paines massif forms a stunning phalanx of weathered cretaceous rocks; 12 to 16 million years ago these rocks were penetrated by granite upwellings that rose through the sedimentary layers, tilting them at odd angles and exposing them to erosion. The famous towers that make up the well-known profile of the Paines massif were visible off to the right as we entered the park. (Torres del Paine has been a national park since 1959; in 1978 it was declared a Biosphere Reserve by UNESCO.) The lower slopes of the massif were cloaked with southern beech trees with waxy, oblong leaves, of which the most prevalent at this latitude was the lenga *(Nothofagus pumilio)*.

The following day we saw plenty of lenga as we climbed up through the Valle Ascencio to reach the moraine at the foot of the massif. The day was lovely, sunlit and mild. The climb was strenuous, straight up a nearly vertical slope that left me gasping for breath. We then encountered a very stiff wind as we trudged along a path notched high up on the west slope of the Valle Ascencio. The path leveled out, clinging precariously to the side of the mountain, made all the more iffy by the whipping wind and a scree of landslides that left the footing treacherous and soft. High overhead loomed a hanging glacier, shot through with frigid blue streaks.

Down below, a milky-green, glacier-fed stream, the Rio Ascencio, gushed along a stone-choked gorge. The water rushing through the constricted passage sounded like an elephant trumpeting through a megaphone. At a rivulet trickling from a hole in the rock wall, Tim paused to take a photograph of the silky-red petals of the chilco, a shrub-like flower that bunches in tropical profusion around the tracks of the springs that dribble from the rock faces.

A display of wildflowers at sunrise near Hosteria las Torres.

We minced laterally across the path of an avalanche flow, where at some point a huge bundle of rock and snow had cut loose from above and plowed down into the stream, carrying everything with it. The footing was dicey, the trail a dim blur across a swath of loose stones and dirt. One misstep and down we'd go into the gorge like a bag of coal on a steep, bumpy chute.

All along the path that wound through the pass we saw sinuous waterfalls fed by melting snowpacks, curling down the high walls on the other side, spilling through notches, lapping over tiered shelves shrouded with moss and leaves and reddish bell-shaped flowers. We passed through a stretch of fallen limbs, trunks, and logs—bleached and barkless, crushed and splintered by rock spills—around which a new beech forest had sprung up. In a clearing I spotted the famous towers peeping up over the final ridge I had yet to cross.

An hour later I approached the top of the moraine, creeping along like a snail weighed down by a burdensome shell. Gasping and wheezing, I came over the top; the view that greeted me rocked me back on my heels. The three towers, volcanic plugs of varying size, granite remnants of a violent geological intrusion, soared up with a majestic thrust from the far side of a milky-green tarn; a squat, massive, thickset fourth, marked with sedimentary striations, stood off to the side, settled on a massive pedestal of chocolate-colored rock. Flat, lenticular clouds congealed overhead, then blew apart under pressure of the ferocious winds. I was so spent and wasted I could barely remember my name. But within minutes my strength revived.

Guanaco.

I joined Tim Hauf on a flat rock overlooking the chilly green lake. The bowl in which we sat was surrounded on three sides by shelf glaciers and glistening waterfalls that glimmered like fish scales in the scintillant light. Piles of loose rock at the base of the towers shook free of the melting snowpacks and slid into the tarn with a profound roar, kicking up clouds of tawny dust. We were sitting at barely 4,000 feet (1,200m), yet we were enjoying an intimate glimpse of a classic mountain scene normally only viewed at much higher elevations. Along with the Matterhorn, Mount Everest, and Mount Kilimanjaro, the towers at Torres del Paine National Park in Chile comprise one of the best-known mountain profiles in the world.

Alongside a churning stream on the path back down through the Valle Ascencio, we watched a torrent duck *(Merganetta armata)* and its mate work the swift-flowing current in search of small fish and insects. The ducks dipped into the water; using their sturdy wings as rudders, they swam through the current, slipping upstream, gliding over rocks, hauling out for a few moments, then diving back in and squiggling downstream.

Next morning Tim and I started out ahead of the others. We crossed a steppe full of hummocky, light yellow, shrublike growths called mata barrosa *(mulinum spinosum),* which grow on high, open, undulating meadowlands. A black-faced ibis *(Theristicus melanopis)* clacked worriedly and led us away from its nest where its little ones were obviously concealed. A rufous-collared sparrow *(Zonotrichia capensis)* fussed around the bright, sticky blossoms of a colorful firebush. Chilean swallows *(Tachycineta meyeni)* swooped near our heads. At one point a sunbeam caught the figure of a local flycatcher known as the fire-eyed diucon *(Xolmis pyropepyrope),* a gray bird with a ruffled white breast and eyes that glowed like polished garnets.

That afternoon we caught our first sight of the "Horns," the famous Cuernos del Paine, lavishly sculpted granite upwellings carved by ice into smooth, figurative, Brancusi-like blades. We passed along Lago Nordenskjold, buttery smooth in the windless air, with a glowing translucent surface that radiated a milky-emerald light from deep within its mysterious depths.

Next day we started out in the teeth of a howling wind on a seven-mile (11.3km) hike, west-southwest along the north shore of Lago Nordenskjold. Our destination was Refugio Pehoe (refugio: a mountain hut equipped with showers, bunks, and kitchen facilities), with a side jaunt up through Valle del Frances. The lake surface, so beguilingly smooth yesterday, seethed and frothed with whitecaps. Directly overhead drifted a pair of soft, whirly, whale-shaped clouds; this part of Patagonia was a phenomenological revel, with natural features warped and twisted by the elements into fantastical colors and shapes. At one point we stopped to sample some calafate berries *(Berberis buxifolia),* quite tasty, with a distinct apple flavor. "Those who eat the calafate berry will return to Patagonia," goes the local saying, so naturally we gobbled them down.

We enjoyed a relaxing lunch break with a fine view of Lago Skottsberg. The wind chewed across the marbly blue surface, stirring a fine lacy spray. I refilled my water jug in a trickling stream and took a long, quenching swallow; how many places in the world can you still do that, I wondered.

Next day we proceeded to Refugio Grey by horseback. There were four of us in the party, accompanied by a gaucho named Fernando. Fernando wore dark leather boots that rose to midcalf, with baggy gray pantaloons tucked into the tops. Over his blue windbreaker was draped a black-and-white-checked kerchief; a knife encased in a sheath stuck up from under a colorful, sashlike belt. The features of his fine-boned face beamed through a sun-stained complexion; a two-day growth of whiskers shaded his cheeks and chin.

Up a long winding pass we plodded, past a burned-out section overlooking Lago los Patos. I was mounted on a sorrel named Paolo—sure-footed but with an annoying habit of stopping suddenly to crop grass. The first time he did this, I nearly pitched over his neck to the ground.

On the level stretches, Paolo broke into a trot to keep up with the next horse. I tried to get into a rhythm with him, bouncing in synch whenever he sped up, but mostly I just swayed in the saddle like a rag doll tied to the top of a swinging stick. The path got steeper and rockier; twice we had to dismount and lead the horses up over some big outcroppings. At the top of the pass we were greeted with an astounding view of the glimmery, blue-lit frontal mass of Glaciar Grey. To come upon this sight in the middle of these lakes and forests was incredible; I felt as if I was hallucinating. Out front of the mass, propelled by the wind sweeping off the glacier, a half-dozen floes, looking like chunks of soiled styrofoam, drifted down Lago Grey in a southerly direction.

Then followed a perilous sequence of trails, straight up and straight down, along the edge of a precipitous drop into the lake itself, my heart clattering like a jackhammer in my throat. The best thing was simply to let the horse have his head, and Paolo steered me through without a hitch, sliding straight down steep rock inclines on flattened hooves and lurching up sharp inclines with me clutching frantically to the hornless saddle.

This part of Patagonia experiences some of the most mercurial weather in the world. Ferocious winds, blowing unimpeded for thousands of miles across the South Pacific, strike the Andean cordillera between latitudes 40 and 60 (the "Roaring Forties"), whereupon they chill and rise, condensing first into rain and then, as they continue to rise, into snow. As much as 200 inches (5,000 mm) of snow a year falls in this zone, more than enough to replenish the low-lying Patagonian ice fields. Drained of moisture, the winds then whip over the dry steppes, chapping the shrubs and grass from the foothills to the Atlantic coast.

The following morning we boarded the catamaran that transported us across Lago Pehoe and away from Torres del Paine National Park. We enjoyed spectacular views of the Horns massif as we cruised from west to east, through a wild, pelting wind, across a bumpy, popping lake that looked as if it was being peppered with machine-gun bullets. The slow inexorable process of shaping and weathering, especially the fine-tuning responsible for the intricate forms and facets of the remarkable towers and spires, has been accomplished in this region primarily by glaciation. Torres del Paine is like a stupendous sculpture garden, gouged and scraped by crunching ice into a dazzling array of solitary erratics, U-shaped valleys, gelid tarns, deep cirques, talus slopes, and massive moraines.

A hiker takes in the beauty at Mirador las Torres.

Patagonian fox *(Dusicyon griseus)*.

Monte Almirante Nieto and the peaks of Torres del Paine, sunrise.

Torres del Paine and Cerro Nido de Condor.

The Torres and Cerro Nido de Condor, sunrise.

Morning light from Hosteria las Torres.

A rainbow following an early morning shower graces Monte Almirante Nieto.

This is how it is in Patagonia; the unexpected is the norm.

RAMON LISTA
A Journey to the Southern Andes (1893)

Preceding spread: Rio Paine.

left: Wildflowers in Rio Paine valley near Seron (Enchanted Valley).

TORRES DEL PAINE NATIONAL PARK 43

above: Valle Ascencio.

right: Waterfall, Valle Ascencio.

Swing bridge over Rio Ascencio.

Monte Almirante Nieto; foreground, notro, or fire bush *(Embothrium coccineum)*.

TORRES DEL PAINE NATIONAL PARK

The trail up the rocky face of the terminal moraine leading to Mirador las Torres.

Dust from a rock fall drifts across Mirador las Torres.

Mirador las Torres.

*The landscape had a prehistoric look,
the sort that forms a painted backdrop
for a dinosaur skeleton in a museum:
simple terrible hills and gullies;
thorn bushes and rocks;
and everything smoothed by the wind
and looking as if a great flood had denuded it,
washed it of all its particular features.
Still the wind worked on it,
kept the trees from growing,
blew the soil west, uncovered more rock,
and even uprooted those ugly bushes.*

PAUL THEROUX
The Old Patagonian Express (1979)

above: Topa Topa *(Calceolaria uniflora).*

right: Lago Nordenskjold, view southwest from base of Monte Almirante Nieto.

52 PATAGONIA

Paso los Cuernos.

Chaura berries *(Pernettya mucronata)* at the base of Cuernos del Paine.

*The ride was immensely exhilarating,
and it seemed to me at that moment that,
without a horse, one could not get
a true sense of Patagonia.*

PETER MATTHIESSEN
The Cloud Forest (1961)

Trail rider.

Above: Stringy wisps of moss cling to the branches of the southern beech tree, or lenga.

Brilliant displays of fire bush accent the scenery along the Paso los Cuernos.

Lago Skottsberg.

TORRES DEL PAINE NATIONAL PARK

Foot bridge over the Rio del Frances.

Wildflowers and boulders at the base of Cuernos del Paine.

View looking down Valle del Frances toward Lago Pehoe.

Valle del Frances, looking north.

TORRES DEL PAINE NATIONAL PARK

Evening color on Lago Pehoe.

Lago Grey, southerly view.

Lago Grey, northerly view.

previous page: Icebergs, Lago Grey.

above: Icebergs, Lago Grey.

Icebergs, Lago Grey.

The ice was here, the ice was there,
The ice was all around:
It cracked and growled, and roared and howled,
Like noises in a swound!

SAMUEL TAYLOR COLERIDGE
The Rime of the Ancient Mariner

Icebergs, Lago Grey; Cerro Paine Grande in background.

Lago Grey, with Glaciar Grey in the background; foreground, people dwarfed by icebergs.

Terminal face, Glaciar Grey.

TORRES DEL PAINE NATIONAL PARK **77**

Terminal face, Glaciar Grey.

Jagged surface of Glaciar Grey.

Icebergs, Lago Grey.

TORRES DEL PAINE NATIONAL PARK 81

Glaciar Grey at a distance from a vantage point overlooking Lago Grey.

In the middle of the lake we see some capriciously shaped icebergs
that sail in the direction of the wind.
We are deliciously surprised by the gothic contours of one of them;
it is almost a medieval cathedral, fantastically lighted by the setting sun.
Another one, farther away, looks like a sailing ship; and the furthermost one . . .
stands in all its majesty, in the north-west angle of the lake.

RAMON LISTA,
A Journey to the Southern Andes (1893)

Dramatic color and light on Lago Pehoe and Cuernos del Paine.

Cuernos del Paine glimpsed through a shroud of windblown rain.

South side of Lago Nordenskjold.

The Paine massif towers over Lago Nordenskjold.

Steady winds whip the surface of Lago Nordenskjold into a curdly froth of whitecaps.

Salto Grande as it pours from Lago Nordenskjold into Lago Pehoe.

Salto Grande draining into Lago Pehoe.

Salto Grande pours from Lago Nordenskjold into Lago Pehoe.

Rainbow over Lago Pehoe.

*Nowhere else are you so completely alone.
Nowhere else is there an area of 100,000 square miles
which you may gallop over, and where, whilst enjoying a healthy, bracing climate,
you are safe from the persecution of fever, friends, savage tribes,
obnoxious animals, telephones, letters and every other nuisance
you are elsewhere liable to be exposed to.*

LADY FLORENCE DIXIE
Across Patagonia (1880)

Torrent duck.

The guanaco, or wild llama, is the characteristic quadruped of the plains of Patagonia; it is the South American representative of the camel of the East. It is an elegant animal in a state of nature, with a long slender neck and fine legs. It is very common over the whole of the temperate parts of the continent, as far south as the islands near Cape Horn. It generally lives in small herds of from a dozen to thirty in each; but on the banks of the Santa Cruz we saw one herd which must have contained at least five hundred.

CHARLES DARWIN
The Voyage of the Beagle (1839)

previous spread: Lago Pehoe and the Paine massif.

Guanacos.

left: Guanacos embrace in courtship ritual.

right: Guanacos.

Guanacos.

TORRES DEL PAINE NATIONAL PARK 103

Lesser rhea.

Lesser rhea.

TORRES DEL PAINE NATIONAL PARK 105

Cascade Paine.

Laguna Azul stippled with whitecaps.

CHAPTER 3

Los Glaciares National Park

THE BUS RUMBLED EAST THEN NORTH THROUGH UNDULATING CATTLE AND SHEEP COUNTRY, WHERE THE LAND flattened out into a sequence of monochromatic steppes. In 30 minutes we went from spectacular mountain country to the dreariness of the pampas. "The land rises and falls more gently now," says Peter Matthiessen in *The Cloud Forest,* "so monotone and lifeless that one has the impression—not inaccurate, from a geological point of view—of the floor beneath the sea." It was a little like how I imagined the American West must have looked a hundred years ago.

At the Argentine border post, a solitary outbuilding plunked down in the middle of a vast treeless steppe, we showed our passports and collected our stamps and wobbled back out to the bus in the teeth of a chafing wind that smoothed the skin on our faces like a sheet of sandpaper. Wind, wind, wind. Blowing, surging, sliding, cascading, whistling, bumping, knocking. The omnipresent atmospheric force in this huge, empty land.

El Calafate, on the shores of Lago Argentino, was a bustling tourist emporium with myriad facilities that cater to hikers and trekkers. The next morning we trundled out by bus to observe up close the famous Glaciar Moreno, named after the Argentine naturalist Francisco P. Moreno (1852–1919). In 1876 Moreno led an expedition up the Rio Santa Cruz from the Atlantic Ocean to its source at the foot of the Andes. The upstream trip took 30 days, whereas the return—on the surge of a swift current, a distance of 140 miles (225 km), through boiling rapids—took only three.

Glaciar Moreno—wide, wavy, S-shaped—sludges inexorably downhill to spill into an arm of Lago Argentino. It covers an area of 200 square miles (518 square km), and advances an average of eight feet (2.5 m) a day; its leading edge measures about 3½ miles (5.5 km) wide. It belongs to the largest icecap in South America, the Hielo Patagonico (Continental) Sur, which stretches about 250 miles (400 km) from north to south and encompasses roughly 9,000 square miles (23,310 square km), mostly in Chile. The entire Patagonian ice field, Hielo Norte and Sur, which extends from latitude 47 to latitude 51, lies closer to the equator than any other ice field in the world. In the Northern Hemisphere, to find large ice masses you have to go as far north as Greenland and Iceland (latitude 60 degrees).

< Fitz Roy massif.

Glaciers are sustained by heavy snowfall accumulations, which pile up in more of a mass than can properly melt. As the weight accumulates, it squeezes out the air and generates the eerie blue light that stipples the ice mass in jagged flashes. The weight also stirs the mass and sends it crunching downhill, to the point where the sheer heft of the leading edge starts to flake off.

The top surface of the glacier, as viewed from the vantage point of the observation platform, looked jagged and rough. The humidity generated by the melting ice helped incubate swarms of mosquitoes and horseflies. The frontal mass of the advancing glacier emitted a chorus of creaky sounds like the hull of a wooden ship. Every few minutes a slab calved off the face of the berg into the cold meltwater with a resounding splash, to the loud cheers of observers like ourselves.

The glacier face was streaked with charcoal draperies; blue highlights splashed the length as far back as I could see, pastel blue to dazzling cobalt, depending upon the degree of weight compressing the snow and ice. "It is scarcely possible to imagine anything more beautiful than the beryl-like blue of these glaciers, and especially as contrasted with the dead white of the upper expanse of snow," Charles Darwin wrote in *The Voyage of the Beagle*. Darwin visited the region in 1834 during his famous 'round-the-world voyage. In the company of the *Beagles'* commander, Robert Fitz Roy, he toiled up the Rio Santa Cruz nearly to the shores of Lago Argentino before lack of food forced them to abandon the effort.

That afternoon we journeyed to the town of El Chalten, located in a box canyon near the northwest corner of Lago Viedma, at the foot of the Fitz Roy massif, whose peaks and pinnacles stuck up against the northern horizon like glass shards from a shattered wine bottle. El Chalten marked the entry point to Los Glaciares National Park, established in 1937 and declared a UNESCO World Heritage Site in 1982.

Tehuelche Indians referred to the Fitz Roy massif as "the mountain that smokes." Early explorers deemed it a volcano because of the veils of clouds that perpetually stream around it. The massif is a chunk of fissured stone spiked with granite spires and stone minarets, fluted and mantled with mushroom-shaped snowcaps, with a massive triangular centerpiece rearing into the air like a steeple. The two most prominent peaks, Cerro Fitz Roy and Cerro Torre, majestic granite spires, were formed when softer layers of rock that once covered these igneous intrusions eroded over a period of 16 million years. Like Torres del Paine National Park, the Fitz Roy massif is buffeted by some of the most violently unpredictable weather in the world.

The next morning we climbed to the foot of the massif. It was a fairly easy hike, straight up the side of a slope and then across a spacious plateau, at the end of which loomed a tall, messy, boulder-packed moraine. The hike included a fine view of the mouth of the Rio de las Vueltas, a wide U-shaped valley crunched out by glaciers. The region was first settled by European immigrants in the early 1900s. The town of El Chalten was founded by the Argentine government in 1985 as a buffer against possible Chilean expansionist attempts; the border between the two countries, a chronic bone of contention, lies a scant few miles to the west. Today the town is flourishing, with new hotels, restaurants, and specialty shops under construction.

In the last third of the nineteenth century, the real Argentine border ended somewhere between the Rio Colorado and Rio Negro far to the north. Patagonia was regarded as a separate land, free to anyone who could successfully occupy it. Immigration remained little more than

Anemone *(Anemone multifida)*.

a trickle, even during the peak years of the late nineteenth century. Settlers from Wales occupied the arable land along the Rio Chubut, while longtime English colonists from the Falkland Islands (Malvinas) brought their sheep over to the mainland to help found what would become one of the major Patagonian industries.

    The pattern of settlement around Lago Viedma was typical of the rest of Patagonia. Small land claims made by squatters were repeatedly challenged by large absentee owners operating out of Buenos Aires who had the money, lawyers, and politicians on their side. The big landowners tried to coerce the smaller settlers into abandoning their plots by fostering evictions without a judicial order, aided by unscrupulous public officers who favored the highest bidder.

    The squatters persisted against staggering odds; when one was evicted, another took his place. Legal possession of the land in the Patagonian outback was facilitated by making definite improvements—planting fields, grazing stock, constructing houses and outbuildings. The land was unsuited for cultivation, the weather was harsh, the chances of survival were iffy at best; but slowly as the years rolled by, the region became a haven not only for hardy settlers but for lonely hermits seeking to hide out in the grassy corners of the Fitz Roy massif.

    The next day we drove across the width of the South American cone to the Atlantic coast town of Rio Gallegos. The space out here away from the mountains was tremendous, the Rio Santa Cruz valley dotted with erratics stranded by the ice flow many thousands of years ago. Out the bus window I watched a trio of guanacos mince delicately toward a rain pond. The guanaco is perhaps the most appealing and representative mammal of the Patagonian fauna. It has a small, narrow head, long neck, pointed ears, cinnamon-colored hair, a black muzzle,

Cerro Fitz Roy, Chorrillo del Salto.

whitish belly and throat. Following the disappearance of the giant sloth at the time of the glaciers and until cattle and sheep were introduced by nineteenth-century settlers, the only major indigenous grazing animal to roam these steppes was the light-footed guanaco.

I spotted an estancia or two nestled in the depths of this gigantic valley, a handful of dirt roads, a few poles strung with wires, microscopic clusters of trees, a faint trace of a fence, a few scattered beeves, a solitary horse or two. Virtually no hint of a human presence, no familiar farm props, machines, or vehicles of any kind.

The sight of an animal or a bird or even a windmill or a water tank is a major event in this landscape. In Patagonia one still observes the world through the conventional end of a telescope; details are magnified under its scrutiny but without compromising the ineffable context in which they occur. You believe the space out here because you can actually see it, because it is virtually impossible to measure (like Alaska) with conventional points of reference.

Butch Cassidy and the Sundance Kid (a.k.a. Harry Longabaugh) robbed a bank in Rio Gallegos. Riding up from Punta Arenas one day, they stopped in Rio Gallegos (pop. 900) and opened an account in a local bank. They chatted up the locals and reconnoitered the best roads leading out of town. On February 13, 1905, they withdrew the pesos in the account they had established; midafternoon they returned to the bank, drew their revolvers, and robbed the place of literally every coin it contained. A posse gave chase, patrols from as far away as Chile joined the hunt, but the thieves were never apprehended.

Clouds often obscure views of Cerro Torre from Lago Torre.

previous spread: A lone car speeds across the steppe between El Calafate and El Chalten, churning up a column of dust. Cerro Fitz Roy visible in the distance.

top left: The Steppe between El Calafate and El Chalten.

top right: Petunia *(Petunia patagonica)*.

bottom left: Adesmia *(Adesmia villosa)*.

bottom right: Mariposa del Campo *(Alstroemeria patagonica)*.

*The Patagonian paradox was this:
to be here, it helped to be a miniaturist,
or else interested in enormous empty spaces.
There was no intermediate zone of study.
Either the enormity of the desert space,
or the sight of a tiny flower.
You had to choose between
the tiny or the vast.*

PAUL THEROUX
The Old Patagonian Express (1979)

Glaciar Moreno.

Glaciar Moreno and fire bush.

Glaciar Moreno.

Glaciar Moreno.

Glaciar Moreno, calving.

LOS GLACIARES NATIONAL PARK 123

previous spread: Rio de las Vueltas.

Rio Fitz Roy.

Cerro Fitz Roy and Chorrillo del Salto.

above: Cerro Fitz Roy.

left: Chorrillo del Salto with glacier.

LOS GLACIARES NATIONAL PARK

Cerro Fitz Roy looms above a small lake.

LOS GLACIARES NATIONAL PARK 131

Cerro Fitz Roy, Chorrillo del Salto.

Cerro Fitz Roy.

LOS GLACIARES NATIONAL PARK 133

Fitz Roy massif, morning light, 4:30 A.M.

Fitz Roy massif, sunrise light, 5:10 A.M.

Fitz Roy massif, sunrise light, 5:40 A.M.

Fitz Roy massif, sunrise light, 6:00 A.M.

Rio Fitz Roy.

LOS GLACIARES NATIONAL PARK

Rio Fitz Roy valley.

left: Palomita–Dog orchid *(Codonorchis lessonii).*

center: Mountain tulip *(Chloraea alpina).*

right: Pan de Indio–Darwin's fungus *(Cyttaria darwinii).*

Lago Torre.

Rio Fitz Roy.

LOS GLACIARES NATIONAL PARK 141

CHAPTER 4

Tierra del Fuego

Ushuaia, the unofficial capital of Tierra del Fuego, has a population of 45,000 and the distinction of being the southernmost town in the world. It's located along the north shore of the Canal Beagle, at the foot of an imposing array of snowcapped mountains. It was first founded as an Anglican mission in 1869 by the Reverend Thomas Bridges.

In 1884 the Argentine Navy established a military presence in the region; lured by rumors of gold, settlers from all over the world began to trickle in. To solidify its claim, the Argentine government built a prison in the 1890s, which for the first half of the twentieth century was the region's primary industry.

Croatian families arrived in the early 1900s, followed by settlers from Spain who started a sardine factory, followed by an influx of Italian families after World War II. In 1947 the Argentine government closed the prison, and the navy took control of the facility.

Ushuaia today is a brash, expansive town, fueled by a booming tourist industry—primarily the big cruise ships that embark regularly for Antarctica. In every part of the city there is new construction, new hotels, shops, and restaurants; although a few tin-roofed shacks cling to the expanding edges, there is no real squalor like that seen on the outskirts of most Latin American cities.

Tierra del Fuego National Park is located just west of Ushuaia. One morning we followed a trail along the shore of the Canal Beagle through a deep, wet, temperate forest composed primarily of evergreen beech *(Nothofagus betuloides)*. A noisy flock of austral parakeets *(Enicognathus ferrugineus)* chattered in the trees—one of the anomalies of this crazy upside-down world, the presence of tropical birds a mere few hundred miles from Antarctica.

The trail along the damp, misty littoral of Bahia Ensenada wound through the heart of what once was Yamana Indian territory. The Yamana traveled by canoe from beach to beach along the inlets and channels that make up this watery maze at the tip of the continent, surviving on what they found to eat—clams, mussels, squid, fish—in the narrow corridor between the beach and the kelp beds floating a few yards offshore.

< Morning light on Ushuaia.

The Yamana are one of four native groups that once inhabited Tierra del Fuego, along with the Ona, Alacaluf, and Haush. Collectively, they are known as Fuegians, and until the mid-nineteenth century they were mostly ignored by the white settlers in that part of South America. The primary cause of their demise, in addition to the usual diseases, was the destruction of their habitat, especially the whales and seals.

Magellan was not the only famous explorer to sail along the shores of Tierra del Fuego. In 1578 Sir Francis Drake turned his little fleet of English ships into the Straits of Magellan; in all likelihood they anchored off Isla Magdalena, where in one day his men slaughtered 3,000 penguins. Sixteen days after entering the Straits, Drake's ship *The Golden Hind* sailed out into the Pacific Ocean, the first English vessel to complete this tricky passage.

In 1615 a Dutch entourage led by Captain Wilhelm Cornelius Schouten beat its way through ferocious winds around Cape Horn at the tip of South America, the first known vessels to complete this arduous voyage. Legendary English mariner Captain James Cook made two trips around Cape Horn in 1769 and 1772.

The *Beagle,* the famous ship commanded by Robert Fitz Roy and carrying budding naturalist Charles Darwin, sailed through the region in the winter of 1832-1833. They off-loaded a trio of Yamana Indians who had spent fourteen months in England becoming civilized, plus an Anglican missionary named Richard Matthews, who intended to settle in with the Yamana and teach them the word of God. The Indians quickly reverted to their natural state and made things so uncomfortable for Matthews that he begged to be taken back onboard the *Beagle* ten days later when the ship passed that way again.

That morning as we tramped along the shore, I tried to imagine Magellan, Drake, Fitz Roy, and other early explorers poking around this confusing archipelago of islets and straits, looking for a sheltered pathway by which they could transit from one storm-tossed sea to the next. The natives customarily lit fires on every point as they passed. To signal them? To let them know they were there? To light their path in that gloomy, fog-shrouded land? Whatever, those fires, observed from the decks of European ships, engendered a myth and a name for a land that persists to this day.

Not surprisingly considering its remoteness, Tierra del Fuego was the last land mass in the world to be inhabited by human beings. It is believed that around 8,000 years ago, ancestors of the Fuegians first came into the region from somewhere to the north. A once popular theory held that the various Patagonian tribes originated from Polynesian sources out in the South Pacific. If they did so it was in minimal numbers, as recent DNA tests on both Fuegian and Polynesian natives reveal little or no kinship between them.

Our guide that morning on the trail edging alongside Ensenada Bay was a winsome woman in her mid-30s with a pale complexion, hazel-green eyes, and a charming smile. She'd grown up in Buenos Aires and followed her boyfriend to Tierra del Fuego, where they married. "I couldn't stand the place when I first arrived. I cried myself to sleep every night. Too cold, too foggy, too far from every other place." She loves it now and considers herself a Patagonian, not an Argentine. "There's been some talk of Patagonia separating itself from Argentina and Chile, but that's mostly a whimsical fantasy," she sighs. "I wish it were true."

At one point in our stroll we passed through an area wrecked by beaver activity. The animal was introduced to the region from North America in the 1940s as an economic inducement so people could trap them. But the pelts the beaver developed down here were too thin to fetch much return on any fur market, international or local. Today in Tierra del Fuego, an estimated quarter-million of these creatures continue to wreak havoc on the landscape.

Next morning, our final full day in Patagonia, we boarded a charming old boat with a wood-paneled interior and parquet floors, Christmas decorations spangling the walls and doorways, and steamed out into the Canal Beagle. Lenticular clouds hung high over the water like stationary disks. A brisk easterly wind curdled the slate-blue surface of the channel into a mass of frothy whitecaps.

We approached a long, narrow rock swarmed over at one end with South American sea lions *(Otaria flavescens),* the males heaped on top of one another like fraternity boys sleeping off the effects of an all-night drunk. The females basked in the sun in a separate group, their pups nursing at their dugs. Sexual dimorphism between males and females flourishes among this species, with the males growing to twice, even three times the size of the smaller females.

The boat bobbed and swayed at the edge of the kelp. The sun glimmered with dazzling intensity. Back home it was winter, but here in the antipodes, where curious animals cohabit in a boundless landscape, spring was about to blossom into summer. All around, the mountains soared up from the floor of the sea, their slopes and summits packed with snow. A polar chill from the Antarctic, a mere few hundred miles away, lingered in the sunlit air. Patagonia is a place where you can disappear like Butch Cassidy, or reinvent yourself like our guide in Tierra del Fuego National Park, or encounter mystifying creatures such as the lesser rhea and Magellanic penguin. Its magnetic emptiness calls forth a commensurate yearning for a newer, fresher, more hopeful world.

Ushuaia.

The next day I attempted to penetrate some way into the country.
Tierra del Fuego may be described as a mountainous land, partly submerged in the sea,
so that deep inlets and bays occupy the place where valleys should exist.
The mountain sides . . . are covered from the water's edge upwards by one great forest. . . .
To find an acre of level land in any part of the country is most rare . . .
everywhere else, the surface is covered by a thick bed of swampy peat.
Even within the forest, the ground is concealed by a mass of slowly putrefying vegetable matter,
which, from being soaked with water, yields to the foot.

CHARLES DARWIN

The Voyage of the Beagle (1839)

previous spread: Early morning, Ushuaia harbor.

above: Senda Costera along Canal Beagle, Tierra del Fuego National Park.

Senda Costera along Canal Beagle, Tierra del Fuego National Park.

Old pier pilings, Senda Costera.

above: Senda costera

right: *Pan de Indio*–Darwin's fungus.

There is one vegetable production deserving notice from its importance as an article of food to the Fuegians. It is a globular, bright-yellow fungus, which grows in vast numbers on the beech-trees. When young it is elastic and turgid, with a smooth surface; but when mature it shrinks, becomes tougher, and has its entire surface deeply pitted or honey-combed. . . .

CHARLES DARWIN
The Voyage of the Beagle (1839)

Stump, Senda Costera.

Beaver habitat and destruction.

TIERRA DEL FUEGO 155

Shoreline, Canal Beagle.

Upland goose (*Chloephaga picta*).

End of the trail, Tierra del Fuego National Park.

Times were very hard in the south. Not in the south of this country, but the south of the world,
where the seasons are reversed and winter does not come at Christmastime,
as it does in civilized nations, but, as in barbaric lands, in the middle of the year.
Stone, sedge, and ice; endless plains that toward Tierra del Fuego break up into a rosary of islands,
peaks of a snowy cordillera closing off the distant horizon, and silence that dates from the birth of time,
interrupted periodically by the subterranean sigh of glaciers slipping slowly toward the sea.
It is a harsh land inhabited by rough men. Since there was nothing there at the beginning of the century
the English could carry away, they obtained permits to raise sheep.
After a few years the animals had multiplied in such numbers that from a distance
they looked like clouds trapped against the ground;
they ate all the vegetation and trampled the last altars of the indigenous cultures.

ISABEL ALLENDE
"Toad's Mouth," *The Stories of Eva Luna* (1989)

Shoreline of Canal Beagle, Senda Costera, Tierra del Fuego National Park.

King cormorant *(Phalacrocorax albiventer)* nests, Canal Beagle.

South American sea lion and king cormorants, Canal Beagle.

TIERRA DEL FUEGO 163

South American sea lions, Canal Beagle; Ushuaia in the distance.

South American sea lions and king cormorants, Canal Beagle.

Channel marker, Canal Beagle.

At night, after the exhausting games of canasta, we'd lean on the rail and look out over the vast sea, gleaming greeny-white, side by side but each lost in his own thoughts, on his own flight towards the stratosphere of dreams.
There we discovered that our vocation, our true vocation, was to roam the highways and waterways of the world forever.
Always curious, investigating everything we set eyes on, sniffing into nooks and crannies; but always detached, not putting down roots anywhere, not staying long enough to discover what lay beneath things: the surface was enough.

ERNESTO CHE GUEVARA
The Motorcycle Diaries (1995)

Glossary of Spanish Terms

Azul	Blue	*Mirador*	Viewpoint, vantage point
Bahia	Bay	*Monte*	Mountain
Cabanas	Cabin, cottage	*Nido*	Nest
Canal	Channel	*Norte*	North
Cascada	Cascade, waterfall	*Paso*	Passage, path
Cerro	Hill, mountain	*Refugio*	Refuge, shelter, mountain hut equipped with showers, bunks, and kitchen facilities
Cuernos	Horns		
Frances	French		
Glaciar	Glacier	*Rio*	River
Grande	Great, big	*Sur*	South
Hielo	Ice	*Salto*	Waterfall
Hosteria	Lodge, inn, hostel	*Senda Costera*	Coast Footpath
Isla	Isle, Island	*Tierra del Fuego*	Land of Fire
Lago	Lake	*Torres*	Towers
Laguna	Lagoon	*Valle*	Valley

Bibliography

Aberhard, Danny, Andrew Benson, and Lucy Phillips. *The Rough Guide to Argentina* (London: Rough Guides, 2000).

Allende, Isabel. *The Stories of Eva Luna* (New York: Bantam, 2001).

Alonso, Miguel Angel. *Handbook of Lago Argentino and Glaciar Perito Moreno: A View of Southern Patagonia with Its Glaciers, Nature, History, Rural Life, and Trips* (Buenos Aires: Zagier and Urruty, 1994).

Bourne, Benjamin Franklin. *The Captive in Patagonia: Life Among the Giants* (Boston: Gould and Lincoln, 1853).

Chatwin, Bruce. *Anatomy of Restlessness: Selected Writings 1969-1989* (New York: Viking, 1996).

Chatwin, Bruce. *In Patagonia* (New York: Simon and Schuster, 1977).

Chatwin, Bruce, and Paul Theroux. *Patagonia Revisited* (Boston: Houghton Mifflin, 1986).

Coleridge, Samuel Taylor. *The Portable Coleridge,* edited by I. A. Richards (New York: Viking Press, 1950).

Couve, Enrique, and Claudio Vidal-Ojeda. *Birds of the Beagle Channel and Cape Horn* (Punta Arenas: Fantastico Sur, 2000).

Dana, Richard Henry. *Two Years Before the Mast* (New York: Random House, 1936).

Darwin, Charles. *The Voyage of the Beagle* (New York: Anchor Books, 1962).

Dixie, Lady Florence. *Across Patagonia* (New York: Worthington Company, 1880).

Graham, Melissa, Christopher Sainsbury, and Richard Danbury. *Chile: The Rough Guide* (London: Rough Guides, 1999).

Guevara, Ernesto Che. *The Motorcycle Diaries: A Journey around South America.* Translated by Ann Wright (New York: VersoPress 1995).

Guiraldes, Ricardo. *Don Segundo Sombra: Shadows on the Pampas* (New York: New American Library, 1966).

Halvorsen, Patricia Alejandra. *Between the Rio de Las Vueltas and the Continental Ice Cap* (Buenos Aires: El Calafate Editores, 2000).

Hosne, Roberto. *Patagonia: History, Myths and Legends* (Buenos Aires: Duggan-Webster, 2001).

Hudson, W. H. *Idle Days in Patagonia* (Berkeley: Creative Arts Book Company, 1979).

Lindenmayer, Clem. *Trekking in the Patagonian Andes* (Victoria: Lonely Planet Publications, 1998).

Lista, Ramon. *A Journey to the Southern Andes: A Journal of the 1890 Expedition* (Buenos Aires: El Calafate Editores, 2000).

Lista, Ramon. *The Tehuelche Indians: A Disappearing Race* (Buenos Aires: El Calafate Editores, 1999).

Lutz, Dick. *Patagonia: At the Bottom of the World* (Salem, OR: Dimi, 2002).

Matthiessen, Peter. *The Cloud Forest: A Chronicle of the South American Wilderness* (New York: Ballantine Books, 1961).

Moorehead, Alan. *Darwin and the Beagle* (London: Penguin Books, 1969).

Nancul, Gladys Garay, and Oscar Guineo Nenen. *Fauna, Flora and Mountains of Torres del Paine* (Punta Arenas: Tercera Edicion, 2000).

Neruda, Pablo. *Memoirs* (New York: Farrar, Straus and Giroux, 1977).

Pigafetta, Antonio. *The First Voyage Around the World: An Account of Magellan's Expidition* (New York: Marsilio Publishers, 1995).

Poe, Edgar Allan. *The Narrative of Arthur Gordon Pym of Nantucket* (London: Penguin Books, 1975).

Primaleon of Greece (N.c., n. p., first English translation 1596).

Saint-Exupery, Antoine de. *Night Flight.* Translated by Stuart Gilbert (New York: Reynal and Hitchcock, 1942).

Theroux, Paul. *The Old Patagonian Express: By Train Through the Americas* (New York: Houghton Mifflin, 1979).

Vairo, Carlos Pedro. *The Yamana Canoe: The Marine Tradition of the Aborigines of Tierra del Fuego* (Buenos Aires: Zagier and Urruty, 1995).